THE INVENTION OF THE
AIRPLANE

BY PATRICIA HUTCHISON

Published by The Child's World®
1980 Lookout Drive • Mankato, MN 56003-1705
800-599-READ • www.childsworld.com

ISBN 9781503816398
LCCN 2016945862

Printed in the United States of America
PA02370   731 2485

ABOUT THE AUTHOR

Patricia Hutchison taught science and history for over 30 years. Now she teaches children through her writing. She has authored several books and over 100 articles about her favorite subjects. When she is not writing, she loves to learn about new places while traveling with her husband.

TABLE OF CONTENTS

FAST FACTS

- Location: Kitty Hawk, North Carolina
- Completion date: December 17, 1903
- Cost: $1,000
- Length: 21 feet (6.4 m)
- Height: 9 feet (2.7 m)
- Wingspan: 40 feet (12.2 m)
- Weight: 600 pounds (272 kg)
- Purpose: to prove a flying machine, by its own power, could carry a person on a controlled flight
- Materials: wood, fabric, steel, aluminum
- Special features: wing-warping control system, gas engine, propellers
- Engineers: Wilbur and Orville Wright

TIMELINE

1899: Wilbur Wright creates a "wing-warping" control system for an aircraft.

1900: The Wright brothers build a manned glider. It cannot lift them off the ground.

1901: The Wrights build the largest glider yet. It does not fly well.

1901: The brothers test 200 wing shapes in a wind tunnel they designed.

1902: The Wrights test their third glider. They still have control problems.

October 1902: The brothers correct the problems by adding a moving tail. Orville makes a smooth turn for the first time.

1903: The Wright brothers build a gas engine and propellers for their airplane.

September 1903: The brothers arrive at Kitty Hawk. They experience **mechanical** and weather setbacks.

December 14, 1903: Wilbur tries to fly for the first time. The plane lurches and then crashes on the launch track.

December 17, 1903: Orville makes the first successful flight. *Flyer I* flutters up and down for 120 feet (36.6 m).

Chapter 1

LEARNING TO FLY

Milton Wright tossed the toy helicopter into the air. His two sons, Orville and Wilbur, watched in horror. They were sure their gift would drop and smash on the floor. To their surprise, it didn't. Instead, Wilbur said, "It flew across the room . . . fluttered awhile and finally sank to the floor."[1] The toy, powered by a rubber band, thrilled the two boys. The year was 1878, and the place was Ohio. Wilbur was 11, and Orville was 7.

The toy they called a "bat" sparked the boys' interest. They started building their own flyers, making them bigger each time. But the biggest "bats" didn't fly. Instead of hovering in the air, they smashed to the ground. Soon the brothers became bored with these toys. They flew kites instead.

The boys grew into young men. A new craze caught their attention—bicycles. Orville loved to fix things. He began repairing and building bicycles. He and Wilbur opened a bicycle shop. His business sharpened the mechanical skills he would need later.

In 1896, two tragedies struck. Orville caught typhoid fever in August. While taking care of his brother, Wilbur learned that Otto Lilienthal had died. Lilienthal was the first to show that a person could actually fly. Sadly, a gust of wind had caught his glider, and he crashed to his death.

Beside his brother's bed, Wilbur started reading about flight. Orville's fever finally broke in October. Wilbur told him about Lilienthal's death. An interest in flying began to burn in them again. They borrowed every book their library had on **aeronautics**.

In 1899, the brothers ran out of things to read. Wilbur sent a letter to the Smithsonian Institution. He wrote, "I have some pet theories as to the proper construction of a flying machine. I wish to **avail** myself of all that is already known and then if possible add my mite to help on the future worker who will attain final success."[2] He didn't know then that he and Orville would be the ones to actually succeed.

The museum sent Wilbur some pamphlets. The brothers read about men strapping wings to their arms. Others flew in balloons and gliders. They studied strange-looking machines with flapping wings, called ornithopters. Most of these inventions crashed immediately to the ground. No one knew why they didn't fly.

Among these failures, some successes caught the Wrights' attention. Samuel Langley flew a steam-powered aircraft without a pilot. Octave Chanute and August Herring flew successfully in a glider. Eagerly, Wilbur and Orville decided to become glider pilots.

Otto Lilienthal attempts to fly with one of his gliders. ▶

Chapter 2

BUILDING A GLIDER

The Wrights realized that the aircraft crashed because the pilot had no control. To solve this problem, the Wrights began studying birds. One day, a pigeon flew past Wilbur. It darted up and down, left and right. Wilbur realized the bird was adjusting its wings to control its movements. The brothers also watched turkey buzzards soaring above the river. These birds rolled their bodies right or left when they turned.

The movement was similar to a person riding a bicycle. Bicycles were something the Wright brothers knew a lot about.

The brothers discovered that birds have built-in flight control systems. They twist their wings and flap their tails. The air bounces off them at different angles and moves them in different directions. Orville and Wilbur thought this kind of flight control might help pilots **navigate** their gliders.

One day, Wilbur was playing around with an empty box in the bicycle shop. He noticed something interesting. If he twisted one side, the other side would move in the opposite direction. He showed his discovery to Orville. They thought about how this would work on an aircraft. Raising the wing on one side would force the other side down. Wilbur called this wing warping. The pilot could turn the craft, making it roll to one side. Would it really work? In 1899, the brothers built a 5-foot (1.5-m) kite to test their theory.

The kite had two sets of wings with the brothers' new control system built in. Wilbur, dressed in a suit and tie, flew the kite in a nearby field. A group of puzzled schoolboys watched. The wing-warping system worked!

The kite moved left and right, as Wilbur commanded it to. Excited by their success, the men began to design a glider. This new kite would carry a pilot.

In 1900, the glider was ready. But to fly it, the Wrights needed a place with strong winds. Wilbur sent a message to the Weather Bureau in Kitty Hawk, North Carolina. He received a reply that said Kitty Hawk's beach was "about one mile [1.6 km] wide" and would give them "many miles of a steady wind."[3] This reply excited the brothers.

In the fall, the Wright brothers traveled to Kitty Hawk. They pitched a tent that would be their home for the next few weeks. Living conditions were tough. Sand blasted their eyes, and clouds of mosquitoes swarmed around them. Orville described it as "misery!"[4] But they weren't discouraged. They set out to fly their glider.

Sadly, the glider could not fly with one of them on board. This dampened their spirits. Still, they flew the glider like a kite, working the control levers from the ground. It flew well, so Wilbur decided to climb aboard one more time. He stayed up for only ten seconds. They headed home disappointed. But they promised to return the next summer with a better aircraft.

◄ **The Wright brothers stayed on the ground, flying their glider as a kite.**

Chapter 3

BREAKING RECORDS

The new glider needed more lift. So Wilbur and Orville increased the size and curve of the wings. So far, this was the largest glider anyone had tried to fly. The brothers returned to Kitty Hawk in 1901 to test it. Wilbur climbed into the glider, lying flat on the lower wing. He held on to the front levers. These controlled an elevator that moved the craft up and down. Wilbur's feet lay against a bar behind him. This would warp the wings and help balance the glider.

He was ready to fly. Two friends from Kitty Hawk helped with the launch.

Orville and the two friends watched as the glider plunged wildly. Then it climbed and stalled. When Wilbur tried to make a right turn, the glider moved left. The men made some changes to the glider control system and launched again. This time, Wilbur made a glide of 335 feet (108 m) with a little more control. Still, the Wrights went home feeling like failures. Wilbur told his brother, "I doubt man will fly in our lifetime, not within a thousand years."[5]

Instead of giving up, the brothers became scientists. They built a wind tunnel and conducted some experiments. Wilbur said, "We had taken up aeronautics merely as a sport. We **reluctantly** entered upon the scientific side of it."[6] But the work excited them. The Wrights built and tested more than 200 small model wings, each with a different shape. They put each model in the wind tunnel and ran air over them. They collected data to see which ones performed best. Now they could compute how big the wing had to be to support a person in the air.

The brothers had all the information they needed to build an airplane. An airplane is essentially a glider with an engine.

▲ **Wind tunnels help scientists understand how air moves past objects.**

But, remembering the control problems they had the year before, they decided to build one more glider.

The new glider had 32-foot (9.8-m) wings. The men performed almost 400 glides in the summer of 1902. But there were still problems. When turning, the glider slid sideways and spun to the ground.

Orville added a moving tail. Wilbur linked the tail to the wing-warping controls. Finally, the men launched the new design. Orville was able to turn smoothly for the first time. The brothers took turns gliding 600 more times, flying more than 500 feet (152 m). They were overjoyed! They had made longer controlled flights than anyone before them. Orville happily wrote home, "We now hold all records!"[7]

▲ **Wilbur lands in the sand after a successful glide.**

Chapter 4

TESTING THEIR WINGS

Wilbur and Orville were ready to make a powered airplane. Grabbing what was handy, they drew a sketch of their plan on brown wrapping paper. They had a control system. Now they needed an engine, a propeller, and a **transmission**.

The Wrights wrote to dozens of engine makers. Unfortunately, none of them could build an engine with enough power to meet the brothers' needs.

So they created their own 12-horsepower aluminum aircraft engine. Next the brothers began to design the propeller. They decided the blades had to be curved like a wing, not straight like a windmill. This rotating wing would lift the plane and move it forward in the air. Using a hatchet, they carved two wooden propellers.

Now they needed to link the engine to the propellers. Their knowledge of bicycles came in handy. They built a linkage system much like a bike chain. It ran from the engine to the propeller shafts. The clever inventors made the propellers spin in opposite directions by twisting one of the chains.

All the parts were built. They were ready to fly! They took the pieces to Kitty Hawk in September 1903. But technical problems and bad weather soon dashed their hopes. Finally, on December 14, they put the plane's wooden wing supports into the fabric pockets. Then they hooked up the transmission. They crossed their fingers and hoped that this would be the day.

The brothers nicknamed their plane *Flyer I*. The craft was too big to be launched from the ground. So they constructed a launch rail out of wooden planks. They called this the Grand Junction Railroad.

▲ **The airplane had a wingspan of 40 feet (12 m) and weighed 600 pounds (272 kg).**

The brothers tossed a coin to see who would fly first. Wilbur won. He climbed into the plane and rode it down the track on a small dolly. Forty feet (12.2 m) down the rail, the flyer pitched up. It stalled and smashed into the sand.

The plane was slightly damaged. Still, Wilbur was **confident** they would fly. He wrote to his father, "There is no question of final success."[8]

The brothers hauled the plane back to the wooden shed they used as a hangar. They repaired it and were ready to try again on December 16. But there was no wind. They decided to wait one more day, hoping it would pick up. Their wish came true.

On December 17, the temperature hung around the freezing point. A stinging wind of 27 miles per hour (43 km/h) chilled the brothers. With winter coming, they were running out of time. But they didn't want to return to Ohio without knowing if their plane would fly. They decided to give it one more try.

The Wrights pulled the machine out of the shed. They raised a red flag to signal for help from five friends who were working at the nearby lifesaving station. The men lifted the flyer onto the launch track. They cranked up the engine. The brothers decided it was Orville's turn to attempt a flight. He swallowed hard and climbed into the plane.

Wearing a suit and tie, Orville lay facedown and took the controls. Wilbur held the right wing to steady the plane. Orville released the wire that held it down. The plane coasted slowly forward and lifted off the track. Wilbur let go.

Chapter 5

FLYING

The wind lifted the wings of the plane. It rose about 10 feet (3.0 m) and then dove for the ground. Orville fought for control. The plane carried Orville 120 feet (37 m). He set it down on the sand 12 seconds after he lifted off. Although the trip was short and choppy, he had flown! Later Wilbur wrote, "It was . . . the first in the history of the world in which a machine carrying a man had raised itself by its own power into the air in full flight."[9]

The brothers took turns, making three more flights. Wilbur made an up-and-down flight of 175 feet (53 m). Then Orville travelled 200 feet (61 m) in 15 seconds. Back in the plane, Wilbur made a fitful start. Then he steadied the plane and flew 852 feet (260 m) in 59 seconds. They had done it! The inventors proved that *Flyer I* could make a continuous, controlled flight. Later, Wilbur was asked how it felt to fly. He said, "The sensation is one of perfect peace mingled with an excitement that strains every nerve to the utmost."[10]

Wilbur's final flight landed with a thud, damaging the wing of *Flyer I*. So the group of men started lugging it back to the hangar to fix it. Suddenly, a gust of wind picked up the flyer. One of the men, John Daniels, refused to let go. The plane spun and tumbled, carrying Daniels with it. *Flyer I* was a pile of rubble. Daniels was bruised and battered. Later he was proud to say that he had survived the first plane crash.

Flyer I was destroyed, but the Wright brothers were still joyful. They had **accomplished** what they set out to do. Orville sent a telegram to their father. It said, "Success four flights Thursday morning . . . inform press home [for] Christmas."[11]

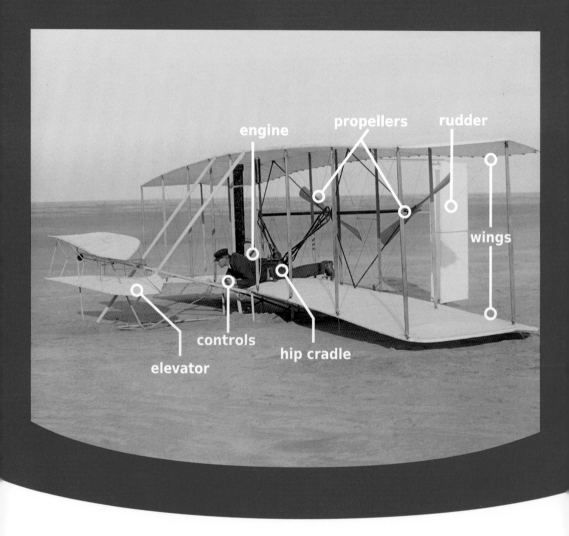

Only five people saw the Wrights make history on December 17, 1903. Others had a hard time believing it was true. Only two newspapers reported about the Wrights' first flight.

Even the government paid no attention. But it *was* true. Many people had tried, but two bicycle mechanics had finally found a way for people to fly.

▲ **A crowd gathers to watch the Wright brothers test a new version of their airplane.**

Chapter 6

CHANGING THE WORLD

The Wright brothers weren't satisfied with *Flyer I*. Back in Ohio, they built *Flyer II* and *Flyer III*. These new, improved models were more stable than the original. Wilbur set a new record when he flew *Flyer III* 24.5 miles (39.4 km) in 1905.

The Wrights wanted to sell planes to the public. But no one was buying them. Some people still didn't believe they could fly.

Discouraged, Wilbur headed for Europe in 1908. Royalty, presidents, and army commanders came from all over to see him fly. In 1909, he received a hero's welcome when he returned to Ohio. Americans were finally catching on. The brothers began manufacturing two planes a month.

In 1910, a reporter interviewed the brothers. They gave predictions about the future of **aviation**. Wilbur was asked if planes would ever transport large numbers of people. He said no. He thought it would be too expensive. He also said they would never carry freight. Orville did predict that planes would carry mail, however. Wilbur never knew if his predictions came true. He died of typhoid fever in 1912. Orville stopped building planes.

Soon, others began manufacturing airplanes that flew faster and higher. Orville's prediction came true when the first piece of airmail flew in 1918. He also lived to see his brother's predictions proven wrong. Planes with jet engines became a reliable form of mass transit by the time of his death in 1948.

The world now seems smaller. It used to take months to cross the ocean by ship. Today, jets make the trip in hours. Long ago, people spent days in trains to cross the United States. Now, planes can get them there in less than six hours.

Orville Wright also saw the first rocket fly into space. Without the brothers' invention, this would not have been possible. But there was one thing he did not live to see. In 1969, Neil Armstrong walked on the moon. Tucked into his space suit, Armstrong carried a piece of fabric from the Wright brothers' first airplane, the *Flyer I*.

THINK ABOUT IT

- The invention of the airplane has had many positive effects on the world. Can you think of some negative impacts airplanes have had?
- The Wright brothers endured many hardships and had many failures before they actually had success with their invention. Do you think you would have kept going if you had been involved?
- What do you think Wilbur Wright would say if he could see how much the airplane has changed the world?

◄ **Humans reached the moon 66 years after the Wright brothers' first flight.**

GLOSSARY

accomplished (uh-KOM-plishd): Accomplished means completed something successfully. The Wright brothers accomplished the first flight in a mechanical airplane.

aeronautics (air-oh-NAW-tiks): Aeronautics deals with the science of flight. The Wright brothers learned about aeronautics by studying birds.

avail (uh-VALE): Avail means to use something that is helpful. Wilbur wanted to avail himself of other people's knowledge of flight.

aviation (ay-vee-AY-shun): Aviation is designing and flying an aircraft. The Wright brothers were pioneers of aviation.

confident (KON-fuh-dent): Confident means feeling sure of oneself. The brothers were confident that they could fly their airplane.

mechanical (muh-KAN-uh-kuhl): Mechanical means having to do with machines. Orville sharpened his mechanical skills by repairing bicycles.

navigate (NAV-uh-gate): Navigate means to keep a car, ship, or aircraft on the right route. The Wright brothers built a control system to help flyers navigate their airplanes.

reluctantly (ri-LUHK-tuhnt-lee): Reluctantly means not being excited about doing something. The Wright brothers wanted to fly for sport, but they reluctantly became scientists.

transmission (tranz-MI-shun): A transmission is a mechanical system that transfers power from the engine to the moving parts of a machine. The Wrights' transmission system was similar to a bicycle chain.

SOURCE NOTES

1. Orville and Wilbur Wright. "The Wright Brothers Aëroplane." *Century Magazine* Sept. 1908. *To Fly Is Everything*. Web. 9 June 2016.

2. David Langley. "Wright Brothers Biographical Overview." *Aviation History Online Museum*. Aviation History Online Museum, 9 Dec. 2009. Web. 9 June 2016.

3. Ibid.

4. "Kitty Hawk: Testing Grounds." *The Wright Brothers: The Invention of the Aerial Age*. Smithsonian National Air and Space Museum, n.d. Web. 9 June 2016.

5. "Wright Expert Interview." *Wright Brothers Aeroplane Company*. www.wright-brothers.org, n.d. Web. 9 June 2016.

6. "Wind Tunnel." *The Franklin Institute*. The Franklin Institute, n.d. Web. 9 June 2016.

7. "World Record Holders." *The Wright Brothers: The Invention of the Aerial Age*. Smithsonian National Air and Space Museum, n.d. Web. 9 June 2016.

8. "Triumph!" *The Wright Brothers: The Invention of the Aerial Age*. Smithsonian National Air and Space Museum, n.d. Web. 9 June 2016.

9. Willie Drye. "First Flight: How Wright Brothers Changed World." *National Geographic News*. National Geographic Society, 17 Dec. 2003. Web. 9 June 2016.

10. James Tobin. *To Conquer the Air: The Wright Brothers and the Great Race for Flight*. New York: Free Press, 2003. Print. 397.

11. "Wilbur and Orville Wright's First Flight." *America's Story from America's Library*. Library of Congress, n.d. Web. 9 June 2016.

TO LEARN MORE

Books

Buckley, James. *Who Were the Wright Brothers?* New York: Grosset & Dunlap, 2014.

MacLeod, Elizabeth. *The Wright Brothers.* Toronto: Kids Can, 2008.

Venezia, Mike. *The Wright Brothers: Inventors Whose Ideas Really Took Flight.* New York: Children's Press, 2010.

Web Sites

Visit our Web site for links about the invention of the airplane: childsworld.com/links

Note to Parents, Teachers, and Librarians: We routinely verify our Web links to make sure they are safe and active sites. So encourage your readers to check them out!

INDEX

9/18

EMMA S. CLARK MEMORIAL LIBRARY
SETAUKET, NEW YORK 11733

To view your account,
renew or request an item,
visit www.emmaclark.org